debbie tucker green

For the Royal Court: *ear for eye*; *a profoundly affectionate, passionate devotion to someone* (-noun); *hang*; *truth and reconciliation*; *random*; *stoning mary*.

Other theatre includes: *nut* (National); *generations* (Young Vic); *trade* (RSC); *born bad* (Hampstead); *dirty butterfly* (Soho).

Film and television includes: *swirl*, *second coming*, *random*.

Radio includes: *Assata Shakur: The FBI's Most Wanted Woman* (adaptation); *lament*; *gone*; *random*; *handprint*; *freefall*.

Directing includes: *a profoundly affectionate, passionate devotion to someone* (-noun); *hang*; *nut*; *truth and reconciliation* (all theatre); *second coming* (feature film); *swirl* (short film); *random* (film); *Assata Shakur: The FBI's Most Wanted Woman*; *lament*; *gone*; *random* (all radio).

Awards include: Radio Academy Arias Gold Award (*lament*); International Film Festival Rotterdam Big Screen Award (*second coming*); BAFTA for Best Single Drama (*random*); Black International Film Award for Best UK Film (*random*); OBIE Special Citation Award (*born bad*, New York Soho Rep. production); Olivier Award for Best Newcomer (*born bad*).

trade
&
generations

two plays by

debbie tucker green

NICK HERN BOOKS

London

www.nickhernbooks.co.uk.

A Nick Hern Book

trade & generations first published in Great Britain in 2005 as a paperback
original by Nick Hern Books Limited, The Glasshouse, 49a Goldhawk Road,
London W12 8QP, in association with Hampstead Theatre, London

Reprinted 2012, 2020

trade & generations © 2005 debbie tucker green

debbie tucker green has asserted her right to be identified as the author of this
work

Cover image: Punchstock/Bananastock

Typeset by Country Setting, Kingsdown, Kent CT14 8ES
Printed in the UK by CPI Books (UK) Ltd

A CIP catalogue record for this book is available from the British Library

ISBN 978 1 85459 912 4

trade

August Wilson
(*1945-2005*)

Thank you
Peace

This version of *trade* was first performed by the Royal Shakespeare Company as part of the 2005 New Work Festival in the Swan Theatre, Stratford-upon-Avon, on 25 October 2005. The cast was as follows:

THE LOCAL	Lorna Brown
THE NOVICE	Nadine Marshall
THE REGULAR	Tanya Moodie
Director	Sacha Wares
Designer	Miriam Buether
Sound Designer	Paul Arditti

An earlier version of *trade* was performed by the Royal Shakespeare Company as part of the 2004 New Work Festival at The Other Place, Stratford-upon-Avon, in October 2004, and Soho Theatre, London, in March 2005. The cast was as follows:

THE LOCAL	Noma Dumezweni
THE NOVICE	Karen Bryson
THE REGULAR	Claire Benedict
Director	Sacha Wares

Characters

Three LOCAL *women*

Also:
The REGULAR *woman*
The NOVICE *woman*
BUMSTER
HOTELIER 1
HOTELIER 2
BREDRIN (*Guesthouse Staff and friend of Bumster*)
LOCAL MAN
AMERICAN TOURIST

All characters are played by three Black actresses.

Names appearing without dialogue indicate active silences between those characters.

/ punctuates the rhythm of a sentence.

(*Bracketed words*) *are the intention, not to be spoken by the character.*

LOCAL 1 *or* LOCAL 2 *indicate '*LOCAL *woman' characters, but are played by the same actress who would play* NOVICE *or* REGULAR *respectively.*

LOCAL	Me.
LOCAL 1	Meh.
LOCAL 2	Me.
LOCAL 1	Her.
LOCAL 2	Her.
LOCAL	Me – mi juss –
LOCAL 2	mi juss –
LOCAL 1	we're juss –
LOCAL 2	'there'.
LOCAL	Local. All a we.
LOCAL 1	All a we three. *Local*.
LOCAL 2	Local to where them –
LOCAL	tek their holiday.
LOCAL 2	To where them –
LOCAL 1	haf their 'fun'.
LOCAL 2	To where them –
LOCAL 1	tek a break –
LOCAL	from who they are. From who they is. We 'local' to that. 'There.'
LOCAL 1	Me.
LOCAL 2	Meh.
LOCAL	Mi juss –
LOCAL 2	mi juss –
LOCAL 1	*we* juss live – 'there'. Local like that. 'There.' 'There' like that.
LOCAL	But them – 'the Novice.'

NOVICE	…What? So what?
LOCAL	Them – 'the Regular.'
REGULAR	What? So what?
LOCAL	Them touriss them: Regular, Novice. They bein that.
NOVICE	'The Regular.'
LOCAL	Old –
NOVICE	She looks
REGULAR	I'm not
LOCAL	she is
REGULAR	I'm not that –
NOVICE	old.
REGULAR	I'm not that –
LOCAL	'old' to me –
	also known as –
REGULAR	depends what
LOCAL	she is
REGULAR	what / what's meant by –
LOCAL	you are
REGULAR	meant by 'old'.
	'*Older*', yes –
LOCAL	The old / 'older' / white woman.
	'*The Regular Tourist*.'
	She bein that.
NOVICE	See.
	Beat.
REGULAR	I think –
LOCAL	see.
REGULAR	I / I / I think to myself… yeah / no / I / I / people that are –
LOCAL	like you

REGULAR	are / are –
NOVICE	like you
REGULAR	are / are / of / of / relationships that haven't worked / marriages maybe – maybe… maybe…
LOCAL	like you.
REGULAR	They're not / not gonna be young… very young / people.

NOVICE *and* LOCAL

    …No.

REGULAR	Are they?
LOCAL	
NOVICE	
REGULAR	Yeh. No / yes… Older –
LOCAL	old.
REGULAR	Yes. I… 'older'. I am.

    NOVICE *sniggers*.

    But at least I'm not… *her* (*Re:* NOVICE.)

LOCAL	The Novice.
NOVICE	What?
REGULAR	You.
NOVICE	*What?*
REGULAR	Least I'm not / no / not (that) –
LOCAL	'that'
REGULAR	that's right.
LOCAL	'*The Younger White Woman*.'

    The first-time-over-'there' – tourist. '*The Novice*.'

    She bein that.

    Her.

REGULAR	See. See with her, it's –
LOCAL	it's the –
NOVICE	iss a holiday / what?
LOCAL	The –
NOVICE	iss my holiday. What.
LOCAL	The –
NOVICE	I paid for it.
LOCAL	The –
NOVICE	*only I* paid for it.
LOCAL	The –
NOVICE	so I can do what I want.

Beat.

Beat.

What? And why would I do – what? Why – what? *What* about me? So what about me – so fuckin what?

Fuck you / fuck off.

REGULAR	Young.
NOVICE	Remember do ya?
REGULAR	See / young
NOVICE	remember that far back do yer? 'Regular.' Does she / bet she –
REGULAR	see.
LOCAL	Do yer?
NOVICE	Bet she don't.
LOCAL	
REGULAR	
NOVICE	And why would I do what I would do at home?
REGULAR	What do you do at home?

NOVICE	I'm not at home –
LOCAL	no y'not
NOVICE	why would I wanna do that? Why would I do what I do back 'here' when I ain't 'here' – don't make no sense – I'm not at *home* / am I / am I?
REGULAR	(*Unimpressed*.) No.
LOCAL	You're 'there' –
REGULAR	on holiday
NOVICE	I am
LOCAL	she is
REGULAR	yes. She is.
	LOCAL *kisses her teeth.*
NOVICE	I'm not 'here' / I'm 'there'. Yeh? Why would I do what I always do? Why would I – would I *not* do what I wouldn't do at home? I'm 'there' / I am / I'm 'there' –
LOCAL	nah mek no fockin sense –
REGULAR	great. I go 'there' / on holiday 'there' / to get away –
NOVICE	from 'here'
REGULAR	to get away from –
NOVICE	'here'
REGULAR	to get away from –
LOCAL	people like –
REGULAR	her. People like –
NOVICE	who?
LOCAL	People like –
REGULAR	that.
LOCAL	People like –
NOVICE	what?

REGULAR	People like –
LOCAL *and* REGULAR	
	you.
REGULAR	People like *you* / that are 'here'.
	I go 'there' to get away from that.
NOVICE	Least I ain't / I ain't / see…
REGULAR	What?
	What?
NOVICE	'*That*.' (*Re:* REGULAR.)
REGULAR	What?
NOVICE	*Her*.
REGULAR	What?
LOCAL	Yet.
NOVICE	Nah – never / I just –
LOCAL	yu 'juss' is juss enough –
REGULAR	exactly.
NOVICE	What?
	REGULAR *is amused*.
LOCAL	See. *I* just –
REGULAR	I know
LOCAL	I juss – mi juss
REGULAR *and* NOVICE	
	we know
NOVICE	I saw yer
REGULAR	I saw you –
LOCAL	mi juss… mi juss / live here.
NOVICE	The Local.
REGULAR	'*The Local*.'
NOVICE	She busy been bein that.
LOCAL	I saw you. Si yu. Them.

NOVICE	'Local Styles at Local Prices.'
	Like your sign. (*Dry.*) I saw that.
LOCAL	'Hair on the beach. Getchur hair done on the beach – getchur hair did done good' – thass mi
NOVICE	plaits for payment – thass you
LOCAL	'the quickest, si mi, Miss Quick Finger – si mi? Canerow fe cash' – thass me
REGULAR	'I don't know…'
LOCAL	'a change a style'
REGULAR	'I don't know… '
LOCAL	(*Dry.*) 'try something new'
REGULAR	'I just don't – '
LOCAL	(*Dry.*) 'live a likkle… iss juss hair.'
REGULAR	'I don't / I mean – '
LOCAL	(*Not convinced.*) 'it could suit – '
NOVICE	nah it couldn't.
REGULAR	(*Not convinced.*) 'You think – ?'
NOVICE	nah it couldn't
REGULAR	(*Not convinced.*) ' – well… '
NOVICE	No
LOCAL	(*Lying.*) 'Y'noh – '
NOVICE	nah
REGULAR	'maybe and like / like / like how – '
LOCAL	like –
REGULAR	'like how Bo Derek – '
NOVICE	like how Becks –
LOCAL	(*Weary.*) like how *we* do.
NOVICE	'Quick Finger.' You do what you do.
LOCAL	Mi do what mi do.

NOVICE	You do that.
LOCAL	Mi do what mi do –
	mi do what mi do well.
	Mi noh mi do hair well.
	Even your something that straight something.
	Straight up.
	A straight-up-and-down… h'economic transaction.
	Like that.
LOCAL	
NOVICE	Like a drink.
REGULAR	Like that.
LOCAL	
REGULAR	Like a meal.
NOVICE	Like that.
REGULAR	Like –
NOVICE	like / see / uh / like like a drink – a drink in a bar.
REGULAR	Like the *offer* of a drink in a bar –
NOVICE	like a meal –
	LOCAL *kisses her teeth.*
REGULAR	like the *offer* of a meal –
NOVICE	like the –
	(*As* BUMSTER.) '*I… y'know – mi see yu –* '
	Like the –
REGULAR	(*As* BUMSTER.) '*Mi see yu… y'noh… saw you from before – .*'
	Like the –

NOVICE	(*As* BUMSTER.) '*I… see yu / saw you from before… and… and tho't unoo was…*'
LOCAL	What?
REGULAR	(*As* BUMSTER.) '*tho't you was –* '
NOVICE	What?
LOCAL	Tho't them was *what*?
REGULAR	He thought I was… (*As* BUMSTER.) '*…nice…*'
LOCAL	
NOVICE	
NOVICE	(*As* BUMSTER.) '*Barman! Mek mi order the lady a…*'
REGULAR	(*As* BUMSTER.) '*Waiter! Mek mi order the lady a…*'
NOVICE	(*To* LOCAL.) A straight-up-and-down economic –
LOCAL	emotional
NOVICE	economic transaction. Yeh?
	Like that.
	Yeah?
	And 'Nice'?
	Beat.
REGULAR	I / I / it's not that… I haven't / y'know –
NOVICE	no
REGULAR	y'know
LOCAL	no
NOVICE	what?
LOCAL	Know what?
REGULAR	I / uh –
NOVICE	(*As* BUMSTER.) '*nice –* '

REGULAR	been called – for… (ages)… haven't been called for… ages
LOCAL	so him call yu –
NOVICE	(*As* BUMSTER.) '*nice* – '
LOCAL	yu let him call yu –
NOVICE	nice
LOCAL	it sweet yu to be called –
REGULAR	'Nice' / I / uh / haven't been called for… years.
	Beat.
	I haven't been called anything for years.
	I haven't called myself / even / well you (don't) / for / uh / for / for… for… years.
NOVICE	'Nice'?
	'Nice' came with the drink?
	'Nice' came with the drink did it?'
LOCAL	'Nice'… ice and a slice –
NOVICE	'Nice' was what did it was it?
LOCAL	Transacted / executed / and accepted –
	the drink. And the compliment.
	Easy.
NOVICE	Nice and easy.
LOCAL	She is.
	Emotional.
	Emotionally easy.
	You are.
REGULAR	I –
LOCAL	Juss too easy –
	(*Re:* NOVICE.) you are.

NOVICE *ups middle finger to* LOCAL *and* REGULAR.

Nu'un nice about that. Is there.

NOVICE	(*Re:* REGULAR.) For years…?
	Beat.
	You ent – 'nice' – not for no years?
REGULAR	
NOVICE	
NOVICE	Really…?
	Really?
	Shit.
	NOVICE *is amused.*
REGULAR	I haven't / I haven't got (anyone)…
NOVICE	(*To* LOCAL.) Ere what – she ain't got –
REGULAR	got… anyone –
NOVICE	(*To* LOCAL.) ere what –
REGULAR	who is there to say it?…
NOVICE	(*To* LOCAL.) She ain't – not for no *years*!
REGULAR	I have no one to say it… So / so why would I feel it?
NOVICE	Say it 'bout myself all the time / say it to myself all the time –
LOCAL	I'd tell yu 'bout –
NOVICE	geddit said 'bout myself all the time –
LOCAL	I'd tell yu 'boutchu self –
NOVICE	gettem to tell me 'bout myself / all the time –
LOCAL	I'd tell you boutcha self –
NOVICE	you wouldn't be who I'd be askin.
LOCAL	Yu askin the wrong people then –

NOVICE	don't think so darlin / but you… (*Re:* REGULAR.) y'know / if you want summat to feel / feel yourself – feel it yourself / you want someone to say it / waitin on someone to say it / say it yourself / say it to y'self – what?
	Y'know / cos y'know / you / uh / I / you / you look… suppose / you / y'know… maybe – y'know / you could –
LOCAL	what part?
NOVICE	You do look… sorta…
LOCAL	She don't.
NOVICE	She could look sorta –
LOCAL	she don't tho
NOVICE	could – nice.
REGULAR	Do I?
LOCAL	No.
NOVICE	Yeh… in… a sorta –
REGULAR	do I?
LOCAL	She don't
NOVICE	sorta 'old' – sorta way.
REGULAR	
NOVICE	
REGULAR	…Should I thank you?
NOVICE	You tell me.
REGULAR	When I need some self / self-help –
NOVICE	just sayin –
REGULAR	when I need some life lessons / uh / lessons in life –
NOVICE	tryinta be helpful –
REGULAR	when I need some advice –

NOVICE	I geddit –
REGULAR	I won't come to you.
NOVICE	
REGULAR	
NOVICE	I just paid you a compliment.
	Or don't my compliment count (then) – ?
LOCAL	As much as his musta.
	Beat.
	The drink.
REGULAR	A drink.
NOVICE	(*As* BUMSTER.) '*Barman! Ah said –* *lemme order the lady a…*'
LOCAL	highballed glass a flattery.
REGULAR	He bought me a –
NOVICE	(*As* BUMSTER.) '*Barman! I said mek mi order the lady a –* '
LOCAL	highballed glass a attention.
REGULAR	So what.
LOCAL	Laced with sweet talk?
REGULAR	Sweetness.
LOCAL	Lyrics?
REGULAR	Loveliness –
LOCAL	loveliness? Bullshit.
	And she *still* looks –
REGULAR	I looked how he made me feel –
LOCAL	*still* looks old to me.
REGULAR	How I felt for once –
NOVICE	once?
	Look like she loved it / ere what / don't she – looks like you'd love it / looks like you love it / loved it.

	Y'look like you landed / landed somethin / and lovin it – ere what – focus on a female's face long enough – can feel how long since she been – 'felt' / how long since you been 'felt'? / How long since you felt / felt since you been – been since you been (fucked) – since she been (fucked) –
REGULAR	excuse (me) – *what*
NOVICE	focus on this one's face long enough –
REGULAR	excuse – no –
LOCAL	(*As* BUMSTER.) '*Yu noh si how yu look "nice"* – '
REGULAR	look – don't –
NOVICE	give it that – and look how this one looks –
REGULAR	look I don't –
NOVICE	you do
REGULAR	don't need you to –
NOVICE	you do / ere what / she does / this one – y'know what – you do / you look… this one looks –
REGULAR	I / I / you know / uh –
NOVICE	– *fresh!* Fresh.
REGULAR	Is this more of your / is this more of *her* philosophy?
NOVICE	Focus on her for a minute –
REGULAR	she can / *you* can keep it –
NOVICE	focus on you for a minute / can see that / can see something / can see someone's been freshly… fucked.
	NOVICE *is amused*.
REGULAR	…The sea –
LOCAL	'bout 'the sea'.
REGULAR	The sea –

NOVICE	thass right / the not bein 'here' –
REGULAR	the sand –
LOCAL	'bout 'the sand'.
NOVICE	Thass right / the bein over 'there' –
REGULAR	the sun –
LOCAL	'bout 'the sun'
NOVICE	thass right / the I gotta tan to work on.
REGULAR	The –
NOVICE	the that –
REGULAR	the –
NOVICE	the what?
REGULAR	The –
LOCAL	the age gap.
LOCAL	
REGULAR	
REGULAR	Before I could / y'know / tell myself –
NOVICE	what? 'Nice'?
REGULAR	Before I would –
LOCAL	'tell yourself' – what?
REGULAR	It does / I just / uh / y'know… he could tell – he could tell –
LOCAL	what hotel you was stayin in
REGULAR	he *did* tell me –
LOCAL	high end, low end
REGULAR	tell me / before I would tell myself –
LOCAL	before your highball glass a bullshit was drained dry he could tell that – if he'd done him job right / was doin his –
NOVICE	job?
LOCAL	Job right.

NOVICE	(*To* REGULAR.) Bitter.
LOCAL	Bitter?
NOVICE	Bitter. Leave her. Go on.
REGULAR	…Before I would tell myself – 'nice' / nice. He… uh / did. And I would / I wouldn't tell myself / that / and that's the / prob / part of the problem / but – and – he could tell
LOCAL	what flight unoo drop out the sky from
REGULAR	and did before anyone would tell me / he told me
LOCAL	package or charter
REGULAR	he told me in two days 'there' what nobody 'here' has said in – years…
	He could –
LOCAL	tell if yu was a credit-card or cash kinda / high-end / low-end kinda / t'ree-week or two kinda / single or not kinda… h'investment.
NOVICE	He could (tell) –
LOCAL	tell if you was German or Canadian or Canadian or English or… English or American –
NOVICE	he could tell you was a (good un) –
REGULAR	do I look American? / I don't look American…
NOVICE	You don't look American
LOCAL	– is what he musta thought.
	Americans give too much –
	(*As* BUMSTER.) '*The American dem – dem gi it too much – too much of the… mout / too much a the h'attitude –* '
	he said.

'*Ent really givin when it comes to givin is it*' is they?

He said.

'*Too much like hard work*.'

Ent they?

And why struggle wid that when what he's got before him is more likely to give...
give it up.

REGULAR	Not nice.
LOCAL	(*As* BUMSTER.) '*Fe free*.'
NOVICE	Not nice
LOCAL	y'not
REGULAR	not true
LOCAL	for the price of a highball glass of su'un sweet then, right?

Ice – slice an' a 'nice' –

REGULAR	it's not like that.
LOCAL	No?
REGULAR	No.
NOVICE	Maybe she's not like that. She said –
LOCAL	before you even finished your first straight-up-and-down-highballed-economic-transaction-of-a-drink / he had you sussed. Sussed – clocked an' categorise. *Thass* what that was for. Thass what you were for.

And yes – 'job' – and *yes* – him could tell –

NOVICE	thass what / ere what – *thass what* / right / what holidays is for. What getting away is for – getting away from it is for – takin time out is for – vacations is – breaks is for – yeah?

Begrudgin me / us – begrudgin us a little a – *I work* – we work –

LOCAL	s'mody employ *you*?
NOVICE	*We* work –
REGULAR	you know nothing about me –
NOVICE	work hard for this – and you / *you* / see / you –
REGULAR	yes, you
NOVICE	you're juss playin –
REGULAR	you are
NOVICE	playin bitter
REGULAR	you are
NOVICE	bitter and backward wiv it – ain't she? – Ain't she –
	REGULAR *nods*.
	and when did somebody last tell you / *you* / see / you that *you* / huh? / You looked '*nice*'?
REGULAR	Yeh.
NOVICE	Right.
REGULAR	Yes.
NOVICE	See
REGULAR	yes
NOVICE	see!
REGULAR	
NOVICE	
LOCAL	When *he* did.
	Before him tell you… that you did.
	Beat.
NOVICE	
REGULAR	
LOCAL	Who paid fi yu second drink?
	Who paid for the third?

REGULAR	
NOVICE	
	LOCAL *laughs to herself.*
LOCAL	Wha? Yu noh haf nu'un f'seh? Cyat ketch yu tongue?
	Or su'un else.
NOVICE	Fuck it / me? I juss took the drink and drank it / so what?
	…Do it over 'here' / so I'm not gonna not do it over 'there' am I?
REGULAR	You said.
NOVICE	Thass right – what? I'm on holiday 'there' –
REGULAR	you've said.
NOVICE	Thass right.
LOCAL	Yu said.
NOVICE	He offered –
LOCAL	who paid for your second drink?
REGULAR	(*To* LOCAL.) Anybody ever offer *you* anything?
LOCAL	Who paid f'the second drink?
NOVICE	He said / (*As* BUMSTER.) '*This is for you.*'
	I said / 'I never asked for no drink.'
	He said / (*As* BUMSTER.) '*Yu not gonna not drink it now / y'know?*'
	I said / 'I never asked for no drink tho.'
	(He) givin it / (*As* BUMSTER.) '*Now that I bought it / bought it fi yu –* '
	(I) said / 'But did I ask for a drink – '
	(*As* BUMSTER.) '*I know yu not gonna do me like that.*'
	'You're blockin my sun – '

REGULAR	yes, alright –
NOVICE	he said / (*As* BUMSTER.) '*You was blockin mi view –* '
REGULAR	I think we (get it) –
NOVICE	'I was tryinta top up my tan'
	(He) gives it / (*As* BUMSTER.) '*improvin on mi view / blockin an' improvin –* '
REGULAR	*alright –*
NOVICE	I said –
LOCAL	I'm sayin who paid for the *next* drink / who paid for your drink after that?
NOVICE	How'dya know there was one?
REGULAR	One?
NOVICE	…Some.
LOCAL	There would be.
	Wu'udnt there.
	If he was doin his 'job' – right.
	Cah, yu h'English like a drink. Don't it.
	Tek a drink. Don't it.
	Like the taste a drink…
	Don't it –
REGULAR	excuse me –
NOVICE	nah I'll deal wiv her – see I – / I'll deal wiv her – see *I* – ain't one a them / ain't one a them Faliraki-out-on-the-piss-out-for-days-out-of-me-head-all-night-type-a-traveller.
	I don't do *that*.
	Vomitin up the place / embarrassin yourself –
	I don't do that.
	In a right state from touchdown to departure –

I don't do that.

Ere what – off your tits – happy to be hungover for me whole of me holiday? See / *I* don't do *that*…

…Any more.

REGULAR *raises her eyes to the skies.*

And *she* don't look the fuckin type –

| REGULAR | er / excuse me but – |
| NOVICE | ere wot / y'know what – trust me. You don't. |

LOCAL *laughs to herself.*

LOCAL	After your first glass a flattery / he ent got no intention a payin fe the rest. Bet you offered… bet him get you to offer – bet you tho't you was offerin off your own-ah back – bet him get you to do that – bet you *said* –
NOVICE	you don't know what I said –
REGULAR	you don't know me
LOCAL	betchu said –
REGULAR	you wouldn't know what I said / she wouldn't –
NOVICE	nah she won't / no one gets me to say nuthin I don't wanna –
LOCAL	yu sure
NOVICE	no one gets me to do nuthin I don't wanna –
REGULAR	nothing?
NOVICE	Nuthin.
REGULAR	Never?
NOVICE	Nah never.
REGULAR	Young. I told you.
LOCAL	Young. She is.

NOVICE	Nobody's gonna tell me nuthin / nobody can tell me nuthin / no man can tell me nuthin / them days is over.
	Where *we're* from. Yeh?
	Yeah?
REGULAR	What – ?
NOVICE	Where 'we' from (yeah) – so don't be sayin 'bout what I said / cos you wouldn't know / how would you know?
	You don't know / see – quiet – see?
	Be quiet. See?!
	Where we are from – dunno 'bout here – *darlin* – but where we been / where we come from / we been thru the women's thing / we don't get bossed it no more – where *we're* from, yeh?
	Yeah.
	We / past all that / we been thru – well – I never went thru it meself / that was more like her generation / her lot – / runnin up an' down the place marchin an shit / we been thru that / you burn your bra didja? Chain yourself to the fences and shit –
REGULAR	What / for / uh / your benefit?
NOVICE	See / bet she did / tits hangin low as she was battlin 'gainst the pigs / bra burnt to bits as she's chained to some fuckin…
REGULAR	suffragettes
NOVICE	I suffer too / we / our generation have our own sufferin –
REGULAR	which were a / uh / different battle to –
NOVICE	I know / history / I know – our history / an' I couldn't be lettin my shit go / my tits go / thass askin a bit too much of the bit too much / but / my point is –

REGULAR	oh God
NOVICE	where *we're* from –
REGULAR	we're not from the same place –
NOVICE	*country* – not manor / no –
REGULAR	we couldn't be from the same place –
LOCAL	glad we not from the same place –
NOVICE	where *we're* from… no man can't tell / can't tell me – we – *us* –
REGULAR	well
NOVICE	'bout our business / and what to-fuckin-do. Right.
LOCAL	Ev'ryting equal – where *you're* from –
NOVICE	thass right
LOCAL	man and woman equal-righted – where you're from
NOVICE	thass right
REGULAR	well –
LOCAL	equal-righted / human-righted – a he an' she same-way-righted / right?
NOVICE	Right.
LOCAL	Where you're from.
NOVICE	Yep.
REGULAR	Well –
LOCAL	so righted / so right / so righteously right-on yu ha fe find yu'self alfway round the fockin world to find back the kinda man you equal-righted right outta h'existence.
	…Right?
	Beat.
NOVICE	…Right / you deal with her –
REGULAR	what?

LOCAL	Right.
REGULAR	Equality –
NOVICE	right –
LOCAL	man is man an' ooman iss ooman 'cept yu noh satisfied wid that – noh satisfied wid what yu fought for –
REGULAR	equal rights –
NOVICE	right –
LOCAL	be careful whatchu h'ask for –
NOVICE	no – now what / see what – now / look – what / look what she's doin – she's lookin to confuse –
LOCAL	noh hard
NOVICE	lookin to confuse the –
LOCAL	noh hard
NOVICE	lookin to confuse *me* –
REGULAR	isn't hard.
LOCAL	Yu there lookin the kinda man you lookin to like / like to like / like likin our man's dem… right.
	Thass your… human right. Right?
	Where's mine.
NOVICE	
LOCAL	
NOVICE	…A fuckin drink / right.
REGULAR	Right.
NOVICE	And I offered cos I could
LOCAL	equality…
NOVICE	I paid / cos I could.
LOCAL	Real likkle feminiss
NOVICE	cos *I* wanted to.

	Cos I can.
	Cos –
LOCAL	'you're on holiday.'
	(*Amused*.) He is good / gotcha thinkin that.
NOVICE	Cos he bought me one first – cos I could…
	Cos I said '*I'll treat yer*' –
	LOCAL *is amused*.
	What?
	Beat.
LOCAL	(*To* REGULAR.) After *your* first glass a flattery… Bet *you* offered… betchu did –
REGULAR	*I* offered because I could.
	I paid / because I could.
	Because I wanted to.
	Because I can.
	Because – and / I'm not / I – I'm not going to –
NOVICE	nah don't.
REGULAR	I'm not going to justify –
NOVICE	nah don't –
REGULAR	I'm not – to you –
NOVICE	nah *don't* –
REGULAR	I'm not going to ridicule the
LOCAL	what?
REGULAR	…Romance –
NOVICE	what?
LOCAL	'Romance'?
REGULAR	…Romance of it.
NOVICE	Get your romance at home – fuck that
REGULAR	there is no romance at home

LOCAL	not our problem
NOVICE	fuck that.
REGULAR	The romance – I'm not like you –
NOVICE	I'm not like *you*
REGULAR	you couldn't be like me.
NOVICE	
REGULAR	When did you last –
LOCAL	walk by the water?
NOVICE	So no.
REGULAR	Stare at the stars –
NOVICE	so fuckin no
LOCAL	(*Dry.*) hand hold?
REGULAR	While he held you / yes
LOCAL	(*Mocking.*) and dance?
NOVICE	Dance? You / dance?
REGULAR	And… yes / I / uh… dance…
NOVICE	Fuck –
REGULAR	when did you last –
NOVICE	that. *Right*. Off. I came to –
REGULAR	do that?
NOVICE	I came to –
LOCAL	fuck?
NOVICE	
LOCAL	
NOVICE	I ain't a one to get fucked over, darlin. Trust me.
LOCAL	What? That how somebody did do you back home then?
	LOCAL *and* NOVICE *eyeball*.
NOVICE	And romance ain't my reality.

LOCAL   You said.

REGULAR   That's you.

                He bought me an unasked-for appreciated drink.

                We ate together – that's me.

LOCAL   Who did pay?

REGULAR   He bought me a – I asked –

LOCAL   who did paid (for) –

REGULAR   that's not the point.

LOCAL   That is the point.

                That was his point.

                Thass business.

                Thass his business / thass good business / ent that good business, lady?

                If thass all the business he got?

LOCAL

REGULAR

NOVICE

LOCAL   What – yu noh able to be the women yu wanna be over your 'there' or what?

                That why you come over to our 'here' is it?

                To be what you think you could be / not admittin to what you are?

NOVICE   Iss a holiday / yeh?

LOCAL   Or you still workin on who you are 'there' / haveta come over to 'here' to flex it –

REGULAR   it's a / (holiday). That's (all) –

LOCAL   tekkin a break from who you are 'there' by comin over to my 'here' – what – you disappoint yourself 'there'?

                NOVICE *ups middle finger to* LOCAL.

NOVICE	Not as much as your mother mus be disappointed with you.
LOCAL	
NOVICE	
LOCAL	You got a mudder?
NOVICE	
LOCAL	She like you?
NOVICE	You ain't talkin 'bout my mum –
REGULAR	Ladies –
NOVICE	she talkin 'bout my mum?
LOCAL	Look like it don't it –
NOVICE	you bringin my mum into this?
LOCAL	Well – *look* like it don't it.
REGULAR	Ladies –
LOCAL	'ladies' where? Not what they call yu (*Re:* NOVICE.) – not what they call y'mudder –
NOVICE	you fuckin / like you'd fuckin / she wants to leave my fuckin mother –
REGULAR	I don't think you should talk about her (mother) –
LOCAL	(*To* REGULAR.) you tellin mi what mi can and mi cyant (say) –
NOVICE	she don't know / know nuthin 'bout my –
LOCAL	(*To* REGULAR.) *yu* – tryinta censorise *meh*?
NOVICE	Mention her again / make her mention / let her mention my fuckin mother again –
LOCAL	mention your fuckin 'what' again?
NOVICE	Fuckin do it – fuckin / go on / go on / *do it*
LOCAL	'fuckin mudder'… mother fucker…
NOVICE	
LOCAL	

NOVICE *eyeballs* LOCAL.

What? You is like her?

You favour ar?

She muss be like her... don't she.

NOVICE

LOCAL

NOVICE   I'm *not* like her.

I'm not.

REGULAR

NOVICE

LOCAL

NOVICE   Why don't you take a break from your
mouth... Yeh? Why don'tchu take a break
from who you are Miss Canerow-for-Cash
/ why don'tchu take a break from your
'getchure hair done on the fuckin beach'
bullshit – and. See. I come 'there' cos I
can.

And I come 'there' cos I (can) – / ere what
/ I come 'there' cos it's beautiful / and I
come 'there' cos I ain't been before / and I
come 'there' cos I worked hard / saved up /
and me and my girls wanted to. *Right*. I
come there cos it looked propah picture-
perfect in the catalogue / and I come
'there' cos it read that the 'locals' is...
so... fuckin... *friendly*.

NOVICE

LOCAL

NOVICE   Iss a holiday / recommend you take one.

LOCAL   ...I would / if I could –

NOVICE   I ent joinin your pity party so don't invite
me.

REGULAR   Why would you want to go on holiday?

You don't need to go on holiday…

You don't need to go anywhere else…

When where you are is so lovely…

LOCAL

REGULAR   Er… / Uh…

NOVICE   I done scuba-dived 'there' / which I wouldn't do at home / I done windsurfin 'there' – which I wouldn't do at home / I been on a boat / which I wouldn't do at home / I ate things / I drank things / I seen things what I wouldn't do at home / and I –

LOCAL   fucked a local

REGULAR   which you wouldn't do at home.

NOVICE   (*To* REGULAR.) Pot. Kettle. Black. Yeah?

And I ain't one a them sand slags / come over 'there' / what? / Come over 'there' / and fuck whatever / I ain't one a them 'different-one-every-nighters' / nah / yeh? I done what I didn't do at home –

LOCAL   what she wouldn't do at home

NOVICE   I knew what I was doin / an' I dunnit / so what –

LOCAL   or didju get done?

NOVICE   Toldja. People don't do me, I do them.

REGULAR   Philosophy. Mind / uh / mind you don't hurt yourself –

LOCAL   Do the drinks tho dontchu?

That's the point / thass my point.

REGULAR   What?

NOVICE   Ere what / I don't care –

LOCAL	thass my point –
NOVICE	care boutcha 'points'. There is no point.
	You have no point.
	She has no – .
	Bitter.
LOCAL	What?
NOVICE	(*To* REGULAR.) See what I said? Bitter.
REGULAR	What?
LOCAL	Bitter.
REGULAR	I moved hotels.
LOCAL *and* NOVICE	
	What?
	Beat.
REGULAR	Because I… (could.)
	Because I… / uh… could…
NOVICE	
LOCAL	
NOVICE	Y'moved hotels? She moved hotels?
	What for? / Summat wrong with it? Something wrong with her? It never had nuthin or summat / never had no air-con or nuthin –
LOCAL	You get –
NOVICE	what you movin for?
LOCAL	Y'get throwed out?
NOVICE	Didja?
LOCAL	Heh.
NOVICE	(*As* HOTELIER 1.) '*Y'know* / *this my business* / *our business* / *our fambily business* – '
LOCAL	yu get – ?!

NOVICE	(*As* HOTELIER 1.) ' – *most of the peoples that come to this place / my place / my place that is our place / this place that is our – h'establishment / y'know / our hotel –* '
LOCAL	(*Amused.*) yu did!
NOVICE	(*As* HOTELIER 1.) '*They is / they are – couples / um / they are married / er fambilies / y'know…?*'
LOCAL	(*Amused.*) Them dash yu.
REGULAR	Er –
NOVICE	(*As* HOTELIER 1.) '*Y'know / I / uh… can't have you here… both of you here.*'
REGULAR	
	LOCAL *laughs.*
NOVICE	(*As* HOTELIER 1.) '*If you're gonna be / uh… doin that.*'
	Go on.
LOCAL	Go on.
NOVICE	*Go on.*
REGULAR	…I moved hotels / what / I / I mean / what / but what –
LOCAL	(*As* HOTELIER 2.) '*Year roun / year roun / year roun – year round we get the / bookins that we get year round –* '
NOVICE	(*Amused.*) 'but what' – there ain't no 'but what' –
REGULAR	I just – we wanted to / I mean / but / what – type of hotel was I in –
LOCAL	(*As* HOTELIER 2.) '*Canadian an' British / German an' British / British an' – year roun year –* '
REGULAR	What type of hotel was I in?

LOCAL	(*As* HOTELIER 2.) '*Nuff a them*…
	…*But. We still – nah – tek – yu.*
	We can't take you. Here.
	Doin that.
	Here.
	Wid him.'
REGULAR	What type of hotel are you in – .
	What type of hotel are you in / that won't let / let their own in?
LOCAL	Dash out.
REGULAR	What kind of place is that?
NOVICE	Thrown out?
REGULAR	What kind of –
NOVICE	thass why I stayed put.
REGULAR	I moved hotels –
LOCAL	to one that would?
REGULAR	
LOCAL	To one that would.
REGULAR	
LOCAL	To one that would letchu…
NOVICE	Don't do them ones what let them locals in.
LOCAL	(*To* REGULAR.) On whose recommendation?
	Beat.
	LOCAL *smiles knowingly.*
NOVICE	I paid to be there / the air-con / the room service / that's where I'm stayin / I'm stayin put –
REGULAR	
LOCAL	

NOVICE	without them stayin over – what – what? / What – .
REGULAR	
LOCAL	
NOVICE	What? You two havin a moment?
LOCAL	(*To* REGULAR.) On whose recommendation?
	(*As* BUMSTER.) '*Bredrin. Tings cool?*'
NOVICE	(*As* BREDRIN, *guesthouse staff who knows* BUMSTER.) '*Tings cool. Busy.*'
LOCAL	(*As* BUMSTER.) '*Yu manager?*'
NOVICE	(*As* BREDRIN.) '*Him cool. Busy.*'
LOCAL	(*As* BUMSTER.) '*Still cool wid me?*'
NOVICE	(*As* BREDRIN.) '*Still cool wid yu. Dollars dem ah talk / bullshit still ah walk. Paid room is a paid room. We gotta guesthouse to fill… dollar?*'
LOCAL	(*As* BUMSTER.) '*Strickly US*'
	NOVICE *is amused.*
REGULAR	He / well / he obviously / y'know… knows… the place / places… better than I do.
LOCAL	Exactly.
REGULAR	We. I. Rented a guesthouse… it was –
NOVICE	what?
REGULAR	It was –
LOCAL	cheap?
REGULAR	It was –
NOVICE	cheaper?
REGULAR	It was lovely.
NOVICE	(*Dry.*) Great.

LOCAL	'Lovely.' From the 'nice' / to the / 'lovely'.
	(*Dry.*) Wicked.
	NOVICE *is amused.*
REGULAR	And how did / I / uh / I'm not being funny / but… how… how did you afford to / *could* you afford to… buy anybody a second and third anything? / Look at *you* –
NOVICE	enjoy the view –
REGULAR	look at her.
NOVICE	Hard currency baby –
LOCAL	look 'pon ar
NOVICE	hard currency (baby) –
REGULAR	you're playing at being what you're not –
NOVICE	and you are…?
REGULAR	You're playing at what you could never be at home.
NOVICE	And you are?
REGULAR	You're playin at what you could never afford to be –
NOVICE	I'm only bein what I'm perceived to be
REGULAR	you're playing at what you can't afford to be 'here' / 'here' / at home
NOVICE	I'm bein what I'm perceived to be 'there' / 'there' / on holiday / not my fault / what?
	What are you perceived as?
	What / see / what? So – cos you have more than me 'here'?
	So what?
	I got more'n they got / 'there'.
REGULAR	(*Dry.*) Make you feel important?
NOVICE	Makes me feel like you…

REGULAR

NOVICE

NOVICE   And ain't that what a holiday is for?

                For feelin better'n you did.

LOCAL   Betta than you are.

NOVICE   – I feel good about feelin good / *you* might
                be feelin bad but –

REGULAR   How is how I'm feeling any of your
                business?

                You know what? It is none of your
                business.

LOCAL   How you're feeling is –

REGULAR   nothing to do with *you*

LOCAL   how you're feelin is *his* business –

REGULAR   and *none* of yours.

LOCAL

REGULAR

REGULAR   Thank you.

                Beat.

NOVICE   Livin like this for the little weeks I can.

                …I like your life.

                Plastic fuckin fantastic fuckin –

REGULAR   it's not about –

NOVICE   pound to the dollar / dollar to the shekel /
                carryin the cash / su-fuckin-perb –

REGULAR   it's not all about –

NOVICE   money?

REGULAR   No.

NOVICE   No?

REGULAR   No.

LOCAL	No?
NOVICE	Heat, hotels and hard currency baby. Least I'm honest.

LOCAL *kisses her teeth*.

Andju can do your that as long as you want. Kiss your whatever as much as you want / yeh?

LOCAL *kisses her teeth*.

Carry on with your that –

LOCAL	I will.

LOCAL *kisses her teeth*.

NOVICE	Cos – he said… 'You're not like the local women.'

Beat

He said / 'You're not like the local women / you're *better*…' (*Baiting*.) Y'know.

(*As* BUMSTER.) '*Not beggin mi anytin and everythin every two minutes…* '

You know.

LOCAL *and* NOVICE *eyeball*.

(I) think I know what he means.

LOCAL	Yu n'noh nu'un 'bout what him (seh) –
NOVICE	don't I?
LOCAL	
NOVICE	
LOCAL	…Him said him want fe study / over inna your 'here'.

Beat.

LOCAL *watches* NOVICE.

Him seh…

'Mi gone go beach / gonna find myself a somebody'

(*As* BUMSTER.) '*Noh matter which type a what touriss / what piece a which kinda touriss / mi a go beach an' find a piece a that.*'

LOCAL *and* NOVICE *eyeball.*

Y'know.

'*Gonna find mi a som'ady / som'ady who will get me to their "here" from my "there" / I am / m'gonna – so mi cyan study…*'

…He was top of his class…

You know.

NOVICE	So I fucked him / so what…
REGULAR	…I would've moved hotels anyway –

LOCAL *and* NOVICE

no you wouldn't.

REGULAR   I might have moved hotels (anyway) –

LOCAL *and* NOVICE

no you *wouldn't.*

REGULAR	…Honest.
LOCAL	Honest?
NOVICE	Honest?

Ere what.

At home / 'here' / a – he buys you a drink / what? 'Honestly' – a – he buys you a drink – a meal / so what? Suited and booted / starters / the lot. He lyrics you / you giggle / you coy it / you laugh / you body language you like him / you like him / you leave / you fuck him / so what?

Honest.

LOCAL	The fool's fockin philosophy –
NOVICE	least *I'm* (honest) – you (*Re:* LOCAL.) say something?

LOCAL	Mi?
	No'un.
REGULAR	What I have / we / uh / is honest
LOCAL	no iss not –
REGULAR	I / uh / we –
LOCAL *and* NOVICE	
	no iss not.
	Beat.
REGULAR	We had a good two weeks.
	We have a good two weeks.
NOVICE	You had a holiday –
REGULAR	I have a – friendship.
NOVICE	You just about have a fuckin friend –
REGULAR	I have a relationship
LOCAL	you're havin a fuckin laugh.
NOVICE	'Friends' don't rent recommended 'guesthouses'.
LOCAL	Not none that mi know.
	Friends don't leave for fifty weeks a year.
NOVICE	Not none that I know.
	Friends don't fuck…
	Well.
LOCAL	Friends don't fuck well / or friends don't fuck?
NOVICE	(*Amused.*) I like you.
LOCAL	(*Not amused.*) Mi n'like yu.
	Beat.
NOVICE	(*To* REGULAR.) And it ain't big. And it ain't clever / so you can cut your fuckin foul language right out –
REGULAR	I / we've been / I've been his 'friend' for years

LOCAL	…'years'?
REGULAR	I've been / I / uh / coming here for years
NOVICE *and* LOCAL	
	'years'?
REGULAR	I've been / uh… coming to see / him / for years… I've been –
NOVICE	rentin-recommended-guesthouses / for years –
REGULAR	I've been coming / back / I come back / I've been back to –
NOVICE	see your fuckin 'friend'.
LOCAL	…For years…?
	Beat.
NOVICE	(*Dry.*) That what a 'friend' is for?
REGULAR	I've been back – I / uh / sending back –
NOVICE	what –
REGULAR	nothing
NOVICE	what?
REGULAR	*Nothing.*
LOCAL	Money…?
REGULAR	
LOCAL	
NOVICE	Shit.
REGULAR	…Because I (can) –
NOVICE	'Hard currency' is it? God, you this charitable at home?
REGULAR	It's not charity –
NOVICE	you this patronising at home? Pound to the dollar?
LOCAL	'Dollar to the shekel.'
NOVICE	(*To* LOCAL.) What do you think?

LOCAL	You still send him back hard currency / or yu did stop?
REGULAR	…You tell me.
	Beat.
LOCAL	(*Dry.*) Nice touch. Says a lot / says a lot aboutchu.
	Says a lot about your kind… ness.
REGULAR	You wouldn't know. You / uh / you don't know / you wouldn't / you wouldn't know / you both –
NOVICE	don't wanna (know) –
REGULAR	both of you / uh / you know / you just – don't –
LOCAL	want to –
REGULAR	know. You don't know.
	Beat.
NOVICE	You with who you would be / at home? You that?
	Know that.
	Know that much.
	(I) know I know thatchu're not that.
REGULAR	Are you the person 'there' that you are 'here' at home?
LOCAL	(*Re:* NOVICE.) Know she's not that.
NOVICE	You 'here'… strugglin to get a second look 'here' / you – who can't buy no attention 'here' / couldn't get it given to yer – 'here' / *you* – 'here' – ain't never asked yourself why you gettin what you getting 'there'?
	Why you gettin what you get 'there' so… easy / so soon / so much –
REGULAR	what?
NOVICE	When so much a that so much / is so much above your station –

LOCAL	what?
NOVICE	(*Dry*.) Sorry to break it to ya – attention / so outta your league – so beyond whatchu coulda clocked – andju ain't never asked yourself why you getting what you got? 'There'?
LOCAL	Yu nevah ask yu'self –
NOVICE	that?
	See. Least me an' he is on the same sorta level –
LOCAL	no.
NOVICE	We the same / same sorta shit –
LOCAL	no.
NOVICE	Someone like him likin someone like you?
	Someone like him with someone like you?
	Know you need to ask yourself that / know you ain't asked yourself (that) –
REGULAR	and what have you –
NOVICE	– *how* you haven't / I don't (know) –
REGULAR	and what have you asked (yourself)?
NOVICE	She hasn't –
REGULAR	or don't you draw breath for long enough / your mouth doesn't stop for long enough for your ears to listen to anything anyone else might have to say?
NOVICE	
	LOCAL *is amused*.
REGULAR	No. Yes. See.
REGULAR	
NOVICE	If I was *you* – know I'd need to ask myself something – cos what kinda one-sided

'friend' – sorry – '*relationship*' you got /
got goin on?

Beat.

I'm *listenin*.

Beat.

REGULAR	…There's a / we have a mutual –
NOVICE	whass he mutualise you back with?
LOCAL	Not y'wallet.
NOVICE	At your age – whass mutual about anything?
REGULAR	I don't need to explain anything about myself to you –
LOCAL	if yu shit worked you'd still be at home workin it.

Wouldn'tcha?

| REGULAR | Or you. |
| NOVICE | You got a fuck-buddy and you know it. |

Beat.

LOCAL	(If) your shit worked you wouldn't be travellin to my 'there' an' tryin to wo'k so'un where yu not wanted.
REGULAR	Oh I was wanted –
LOCAL	whatchu had was wanted – not whatchu is / truss mi –
REGULAR	how would you know?
LOCAL	If yu handled y'self right you'd still be at home rightin it – wu'dn'tcha? Truss mi.
NOVICE	Yeh she would
LOCAL	white woman over 'there' on her own at your age / say again what it was yu ha fi bring to the table…?

REGULAR	How would you know?
	Because… You seem to be the last to / to know / I don't mean to be… but you *do* seem to / to be the last / to know.
	About a lot of things.
	Beat.
	Don't you.
REGULAR	
LOCAL	
LOCAL	Is what yu tink him sees in yu?
REGULAR	
LOCAL	Is what it is yu tink *anybody* could see in yu?
REGULAR	
LOCAL	
LOCAL	*Really?*
REGULAR	
LOCAL	(*To* NOVICE.) And yu tink him see – *what?* – In yu?
NOVICE	
REGULAR	Keep telling yourself that. If you need to.
REGULAR	
LOCAL	
NOVICE	See. I had a thing / a me-and-he thing
REGULAR	a fucking-about thing
NOVICE	I bought the drinks
	I hired the rental
	He'd show me the sights / I'd take the view / so what
LOCAL	while he was taking time-outs with / her.

NOVICE	
LOCAL	That part a yu ting?
NOVICE	I didn't –
REGULAR	part of your 'so what' thing?
NOVICE	I didn't know about –
REGULAR	you're no different
NOVICE	I didn't know about you.
LOCAL	Didju know 'bout me?
NOVICE	Why would I ask?
REGULAR	You're no different –
NOVICE	to who?
LOCAL	To her.
REGULAR	I'm not like her / she's like them / those sand / beach / barely –
NOVICE	I'm not (like) –
REGULAR	barely clothed brazen things –
NOVICE	no! I'm *not* them
REGULAR	*I'm* not them.
NOVICE	You're a –
REGULAR	liar.
NOVICE	And you / we know it –
REGULAR	*liar.*
NOVICE	Liar? *Hypocrite*.
REGULAR	Hypocrite? – Prostitute
NOVICE	prostitute? – Whore.
REGULAR	Whore –
LOCAL	*tourist*.
	Beat.
NOVICE	How much respect he got for himself?

	How much respect you got for his self then?
	How much respect you got for *him*, Local?
	Shame.
	Beat.
	Where's your man?
	Where's your man at?
	Shame.
REGULAR	Where is he?
	Beat.
NOVICE	*That's* my answer.
REGULAR	Shame.
NOVICE	Right.
	Shame.
	Right shame.
	(*Baiting.*) You must be well proud / well prouda him.
REGULAR	(*Dry.*) You must be proud.
NOVICE	You must feel great.
REGULAR	(*Dry.*) You must feel *great*.
NOVICE	He must feel great / feel great about himself…
	Feel great about you / I bet.
REGULAR	I bet.
	(*As a* LOCAL MAN *looking* BUMSTER *up and down.*) '…*Koo-ya… Y'lookin sharp.*
	Inna yu "fresh an' fancy" tings…
	A joke mi ah joke.
	How's Mummy / fambily?
	Y'woman.
	Beat.

Prouda their bwoy?

Know their bwoy…?

Know where their bwoy get him "fresh and fancy" tings from?

Nah. Mi nah tink so.

Shame.'

Beat.

LOCAL	Did he even tell you about me?
REGULAR	What is there to say about you?
	What do you have to say?
NOVICE	'Plaits for payment' / 'Canerow for cash'
REGULAR	that's you
NOVICE	'beauty on the beach' / 'shekels for a style'
REGULAR	that's you –

NOVICE *kisses her teeth badly trying to mock LOCAL as she had done it.*

that's you.

NOVICE	And by the way / you plait too tight.
LOCAL	Your scalp's too soft.
NOVICE	You're too rough.
LOCAL	And you're too easy.
NOVICE	
REGULAR	And why would I want to know about a woman that lets her man / fuck / other women… what would that make me? What does that make you?
LOCAL	
REGULAR	What does that say about you?
LOCAL	
NOVICE	I wouldn'ta said nuthin boutchu neither
LOCAL	you ask 'bout me?

REGULAR	I wouldn't have said anything if I was you.
NOVICE	I wouldn'ta said nuthin if I was you –
LOCAL	did yu ask over me
NOVICE	you don't come outta it lookin that lively do yer?
REGULAR	You don't come out of this looking that good.
LOCAL	…Did you ask…?
NOVICE	…I like your sign.
	Beat.
	(*Dry.*) I do like your sign.
	'*Local Styles at Local Prices.*'
	(*Dry.*) Lovely. Look what you got.
	Look what you got.
	…Lovely.
LOCAL	Mi? Mi nah work the beach –
NOVICE	(*Dry.*) hmm lovely –
LOCAL	don't have to work the beach –
REGULAR	(*Dry.*) lovely.
LOCAL	Don't have to tout for the trade. People see the sign / see *that* sign / an' people come to me now.
	People like… *you*.
NOVICE	(*Dry.*) Business is boomin.
LOCAL	No / business is *better*.
	'*It could suit –* '
REGULAR	(*As* AMERICAN TOURIST.) '*Y'know I don't know…*'
LOCAL	'*A change a style*'
REGULAR	(*As* AMERICAN TOURIST.) '*What did you say?*'

LOCAL	'*Live a likkle –* '
REGULAR	(*As* AMERICAN TOURIST.) '*I dunno –* '
LOCAL	'*y'noh it could –* '
REGULAR	(*As* AMERICAN TOURIST.) '*…Well…*'
LOCAL	'*Go on.*'
REGULAR	(*As* AMERICAN TOURIST.) '*Well –* *Y'know – like – could you – like / like…* *you could make me look like / like how –* *Bo Derek –* '
LOCAL	you saw the sign / saw the sign / that sign / you stopped / you did / you stepped up. Thass what I got.
NOVICE	(*Dry.*) That much.
LOCAL	More'n you got.
REGULAR	I don't think so. Dear.
LOCAL	And he paid. Him did pay.
REGULAR	
LOCAL	*He* did paid.
NOVICE	For what?
LOCAL	
NOVICE	…For what?
LOCAL	For the… '*Local Styles at Local Prices.*' For the sign… For the shelter. For me. Fe us.
REGULAR	He –
NOVICE	paid…
REGULAR	
REGULAR	
NOVICE	With what? *Beat.*

	Nervous now entcha.
	What's your sent-back-hard-earned hard currency been spent on…?
	I wonder.
LOCAL	I wouldn't be buyin a second and third drink of anythin for no man I don't know
NOVICE	I wouldn't fuck women off the beach I didn't know / but he did / does / with some old –
REGULAR	I'm not that old –
NOVICE	And where is he… where is he now?
LOCAL	Not 'here'.
	…Over your 'there'.
REGULAR	
NOVICE	Obviously not with you
LOCAL	or you.
NOVICE	I wouldn't want him.
	So, what does that make you?
	NOVICE *is amused*.
	When did he last send some 'shekels' back / back to you?
LOCAL	
NOVICE	
NOVICE	(*To* LOCAL.) When did he last say he was coming back?
	Back to you?
	NOVICE *is amused*.
	I'm glad I ain't you.
REGULAR	(*Re:* LOCAL.) I'm glad I'm not you.
LOCAL	I wouldn't wanna be yous.
REGULAR	Shame.

LOCAL	Yu n'noh about shame an yu n'noh 'bout me / yu n'noh 'bout me an' he.
	…You wouldn't know 'bout them tings deyah…
	A big people ting.
	…You wouldn't know 'bout that…
	The me-an'-the-he is a long-term ting.
	This is a long-term ting / y'unnerstand?
	The we of it / is inna long (term) / lissen – me-an'-the-he of it is long-term tings / me and he been long-term from time / truss me.
	A trust ting.
	Truss mi.
REGULAR	Want to know about my trust?
NOVICE	No.
REGULAR	How much I trust?
LOCAL	No.
REGULAR	How much I trusted him?
NOVICE *and* LOCAL	
	No.
LOCAL	We… Wid no one else.
	Before we was –
NOVICE	what?
LOCAL	We never –
NOVICE	never did what?
LOCAL	Either a we / wid no one else…
NOVICE REGULAR	
LOCAL	I ask him.
	Yu noh.
	Y'unnerstan…

	Truss that.
	Truss mi.
	We truss that much…
	I ask him an' him prove – how much / how true / juss what –
REGULAR	what?
LOCAL	What kinda (truss) / we have.
	Truss mi.
	We never did / y'noh… bare-back / bare-back it / y'noh / flesh to flesh it / y'noh / wid nobody but we self / before.
	Beat.
	An' iss good.
	Feels… well – *feels* – y'nah?
	Yu n'noh.
	Yu n'noh 'bout them tings / a big people tings mi ah chat 'bout / a long-term ting mi a chat / a mi and he ting mi –
NOVICE	bare-back.
REGULAR	Bare-back?
NOVICE	I wouldn't bare-back with nobody, babe.
LOCAL	See.
NOVICE	'Trust me.' Don't trust nobody, babe.
LOCAL	See.
NOVICE	Not that much.
	Flesh to flesh? Forget that. Buy my own – bring my own – British Kitemark the works / mark my words –
LOCAL	thass yu.
NOVICE	That's me.
LOCAL	Young.

NOVICE	Young. That's me.
LOCAL	Yu mother teach yu that?
	Beat.
NOVICE	My mother taught me…
LOCAL	
NOVICE	
REGULAR	
NOVICE	
REGULAR	
NOVICE	What?
REGULAR	
NOVICE	What? What's the matter with (you) – nah –
REGULAR	
NOVICE	…Nah?
LOCAL	What?
REGULAR	
NOVICE	No you didn't…
LOCAL	
REGULAR	
REGULAR	…Do you want to know how much I trusted…?
LOCAL	
REGULAR	
LOCAL	…No…
	Pause.
NOVICE	…*We* always / *I* always / we always *used* –
LOCAL *and* REGULAR	
	shut up.
	Beat.

LOCAL	…You come 'there'.
	…Invite yuself to my 'there'.
	We ask yu / we trouble yu?
NOVICE	So what we can't go on holiday now? Don't think so –
LOCAL	we never trouble yu / never asked yu –
NOVICE	that whatchu want? Can't go nowhere without your say-so / don't think so / shit – no one would be goin nowhere –
LOCAL	iss what kinda holiday yu lookin?
NOVICE	Thass our business.
LOCAL	You juss made it mine.
	She juss made it mine.
	Bare-back.
REGULAR	
LOCAL	
LOCAL	…Bess not be bringin your duttiness to my door.
	Beat.
REGULAR	Likewise.
LOCAL	*What?*
REGULAR	
NOVICE	Ooh… Who is fuckin who?
REGULAR	
LOCAL	
NOVICE	And who's bein fucked (over) – ?
REGULAR	Will you just –
NOVICE	been fucked over
REGULAR	be quiet.
	Long pause.

LOCAL	
REGULAR	
NOVICE	
LOCAL	Old…
NOVICE	you look
REGULAR	I am
LOCAL	she is
NOVICE	she's not that –
REGULAR	old.
	I am.
LOCAL	'*The Regular Tourist*.'
	The 'older white woman'.
	She been bein that.
REGULAR	I / I / I think to myself… people that are… are of… they're not gonna be young – very young / people.
	'Older.' Yes. I am. I feel… old.
LOCAL	'*The Novice*.'
NOVICE	Iss a holiday.
LOCAL	The Younger White Woman.
	'*The Younger White Woman*.'
	She been bein that.
NOVICE	*My* holiday.
REGULAR	She paid for it.
NOVICE	*Only* I paid for it.
	So I can do what I want –
REGULAR	and did.
NOVICE	I didn't know about you.
REGULAR	How does it feel?

NOVICE *and* REGULAR
        …'*The Local*.'

NOVICE, REGULAR *and* LOCAL
        The Locals.

LOCAL	Me.
LOCAL 1	…Meh.
LOCAL 2	…Me.
LOCAL 1	Her.
LOCAL 2	Her.
LOCAL	Me – mi juss –
LOCAL 2	mi juss –
LOCAL 1	we juss –
LOCAL 2	'there'.
LOCAL	Local. All a we. All a we three.
LOCAL 1	*Local*.
LOCAL 2	Local to where them –
LOCAL	tek them holiday.
LOCAL 2	To where them –
LOCAL 1	haf their 'fun'.
LOCAL 2	To where them –
LOCAL 1	tek a break –
LOCAL	from who they is.
	We 'local' to that. 'There.'
LOCAL 2	Me.
LOCAL 1	Meh.
LOCAL	Mi juss –
LOCAL 2	mi juss –
LOCAL 1	we juss live 'there'.
LOCAL	Local like that. 'There.'
LOCAL 2	'There' like that.

LOCAL   I just –

LOCAL 1   mi know –

LOCAL   I just live –

LOCAL 1 *and* LOCAL 2
                     we know

LOCAL   we just... live / live here.

LOCAL 2

LOCAL

LOCAL 1

                     End.

generations

generations was first performed as a Platform performance at the National Theatre, London, on 30 June 2005. The cast was as follows:

GRANDDAD	Jeffrey Kissoon
NANA	Golda John
MAMA	Rakie Ayola
DAD	Danny Sapani
GIRLFRIEND (OLDER SISTER)	Sharlene Whyte
JUNIOR SISTER	Nikki Amuka-Bird
BOYFRIEND	Seun Shote

With members of the African Voices Choir

Director	Sacha Wares

Characters

BOYFRIEND
GIRLFRIEND (*Older Sister*)
JUNIOR SISTER
MAMA
DAD
NANA
GRANDDAD
…*and a* CHOIR

All characters are Black South Africans. Nana and Granddad are Mama's parents.

The conversations are fluid and constant, although some may be happening in different time frames between certain characters.

Names without dialogue indicate active silences between those characters.

/ marks where dialogue starts to overlap.

The choir/live vocals should start prior to, then underscore parts of the text. A Black South African choir would be great.

Pre-show songs used in 2007: As audience enter the choir sing:

'X'Ethewabonakala', 'Dlamini', 'Digkomo', 'Thongo Lam', 'Noikhokhele', 'The Ameni'.

Pre-show songs were not laments.

Pre-show songs may be changed but should be traditional Black South African content, not sung in English.

Prologue: The Names

Onstage CHOIR *sing with the following names called out, repeated and lamented over. They are not singing in English. (You may or may not get through the list – or may need to repeat it…)*

1. *Sabata*	*'Sabata': Another leaves us, another has gone.*
2. *Ketso*	*'Ketso': Another leaves us, another has gone.*
3. *Oliver*	*'Oliver': Another leaves us, another has gone.*
4. *Josiah*	*'Josiah' (Etc.)*
5. *Kobie*	*'Kobie'*
6. *Clements*	*'Clements'*
7. *Jongilizwe*	*'Jongilizwe'*
8. *Nyathi*	*'Nyathi'*
9. *George*	*'George'*
10. *Moses*	*'Moses'*
11. *Bernard*	*'Bernard'*
12. *Bantu*	*'Bantu'*
13. *TJ*	*'TJ'*
14. *Leonora*	*'Leonora'*
15. *Mama Gee*	*'Mama Gee'*
16. *Nomafu*	*'Nomafu'*
17. *Maulvi*	*'Maulvi'*
18. *Selma*	*'Selma'*
19. *Kolane*	*'Kolane'*
20. *Zwelibhangile*	*'Zwelibhangile'*

21. *Kwezi*   *'Kwezi'*

22. *Mary*   *'Mary'*

23. *Ludwe*   *'Ludwe'*

24. *Patricia*   *'Patricia'*

25. *Dumisani*   *'Dumisani'*

26. *Kolade*   *'Kolade'*

27. *Mannie*   *'Mannie'*

28. *Elias*   *'Elias'*

29. *Solomon*   *'Solomom'*

30. *Nana*   *'Nana'*

31. *Potlako*   *'Potlako'*

32. *Lindiwe*   *'Lindiwe'*

33. *Mpho*   *'Mpho'*

34. *Duma*   *'Duma'*

35. *Phyllis*   *'Phyllis'*

36. *Sefako*   *'Sefako'*

37. *Zaccheus*   *'Zaccheus'*

38. *Leleti*   *'Leleti'*

39. *Nkosana*   *'Nkosana'*

40. *Vanessa*   *'Vanessa'*

41. *Lerato*   *'Lerato'*

42. *Nthato*   *'Nthato'*

43. *Zachariah*   *'Zachariah'*

44. *Ambrose*   *'Ambrose'*

45. *Celie*   *'Celie'*

46. *Tsepo*   *'Tsepo'*

47. *Robert*   *'Robert'*

48. *Kipizane*   *'Kipizane'*

49. *Nandi*   *'Nandi'*

50. *Tebogo*   *'Tebogo'*

51. *Nkululeko*   *'Nkululeko'*

52. *Siboniso*   *'Siboniso'*

53. *Duma*   *'Duma'*

54. *Deliwe*   *'Deliwe'*

55. *Thandani*   *'Thandani'*

56. *Anele*   *'Anele'*

57. *Xolani Nkosi Johnson*
                    'Xolani Nkosi Johnson'

58. *Makgatho Mandela*
                    'Makgatho Mandela'

Scene One

The lament and the list of names continues from Prologue. The names fade, leaving the wordless melody only.

The melody stops. Snap into:

GIRLFRIEND   Askin me –

JNR SISTER   he asked her –

GIRLFRIEND   he asked me if / I –

JNR SISTER   Mama, he asked her if she / could –

GIRLFRIEND   askin me if I could –

BOYFRIEND   ' – able.
You are.
You are – able.'

JNR SISTER   Able?

GIRLFRIEND   Thinks he can ask me

JNR SISTER   thinks he can sweet you –

GIRLFRIEND   thinks he can sweetmouth me with:

JNR SISTER   sweetmouth her with –

BOYFRIEND   'you are – you is – you do – you able – you
look you look like you able – to have the
ability the capability the capacity, the
complete… about you – '

JNR SISTER   to what –

BOYFRIEND   'to… to…'

GIRLFRIEND   'to what?'

JNR SISTER   That's not gonna work.

GIRLFRIEND   He thinks that's going to work?

JNR SISTER   Mama, he asked her if she could cook

BOYFRIEND	' – the aptitude the talent the touch.'
GIRLFRIEND	'The touch?'
BOYFRIEND	'The – you are – you is – you do – you do got – the touch… The lightness of touch – the sweetness of touch – sweetness of your touch – the talent to touch a little – '
JNR SISTER	oh God –
BOYFRIEND	'touch a little of – '
GIRLFRIEND	'oh God – '
BOYFRIEND	'of sweetness… You do – you is – you are – look at you… Look how – look how *sweet* – how sweet the touch – '
JNR SISTER	is this workin?
BOYFRIEND	'How sweet that would – touch – '
GIRLFRIEND	'*what*?'
BOYFRIEND	'your touch would – '
	JNR SISTER *kisses her teeth*.
BOYFRIEND	' – could that… taste…The composure – '
JNR SISTER	'what did he say?'
BOYFRIEND	'The control – '
JNR SISTER	'don't mind him – '
MAMA	he asked you if you could cook?
BOYFRIEND	'The calm, the control, the composure you contain – '
JNR SISTER	to what?
BOYFRIEND	'The capabilities you must have – '
GIRLFRIEND	'to what?'
BOYFRIEND	'To carry out your – '
JNR SISTER	oh God

BOYFRIEND	'your – culinary…'
MAMA	Oh God
BOYFRIEND	'to – *cook*.'
DAD	I asked you if you could cook –
MAMA	you knew I could cook –
DAD	can she / cook?
JNR SISTER	I can cook
MAMA	which is why you asked me – you knew – he knew –
DAD	she can't cook
MAMA	you knew. Why did you ask? He knew – he knew before he asked – he asked because he did know –
JNR SISTER	Dada, I can.
MAMA	Mama ask him –
NANA	why did you ask?
DAD	She looked like she could eat.
	GRANDDAD *is amused*.
MAMA	*That's* your father
DAD	a well-fed woman. *That's* my wife.
NANA	*My* daughter –
GRANDDAD	our well-fed daughter.
JNR SISTER	I can cook
DAD	but can she?
	GIRLFRIEND *says nothing*.
JNR SISTER	She can't
DAD	she doesn't cook.
JNR SISTER	She won't cook.
MAMA	I coached her to cook.

JNR SISTER	I coached her to cook.
MAMA	Coached them to cook.
DAD	Why doesn't she cook?
JNR SISTER	Cos she can't –
GIRLFRIEND	Mama cooks. I eat. Mama cooks, what I eat.
MAMA	They learnt their cooking capabilities from me.
NANA	*I* coached you to cook –
MAMA	I –
NANA	I did. I was the cooker – you was the cookless – I was the cooker who coached the cookless. I coached you to / cook –
GRANDDAD	You couldn't cook.
GIRLFRIEND	Nana couldn't cook?
DAD	Your mother couldn't / cook?
MAMA	Course she could cook –
NANA	– I couldn't cook?
MAMA	Mama could cook
NANA	I couldn't / cook?
MAMA	Dada, Mama could cook. Course she could cook – she coached me – and he knows it
GRANDDAD	you couldn't cook either.
GIRLFRIEND JNR SISTER	
GRANDDAD	I coached her. I coached her too. *That's* your mother.
JNR SISTER	Mama couldn't cook?
MAMA	Shut up.
GRANDDAD	She was a bad learner.

NANA	…Don't mind him. Don't pay him no mind.
MAMA	
NANA	
MAMA	
GIRLFRIEND	He asked me if I could cook, Mama –
GRANDDAD	he asked *her* – if she could *cook*?
	GRANDDAD *is amused*.
MAMA	This is how they start –
NANA	oh.
JNR SISTER	Sis, 'this is how they start'
DAD	have to start somewhere –
MAMA	oh.
	GRANDDAD *laughs*.
	This is how your father started with me.
NANA	This is how your father started with me.
MAMA	This is how your father flirted with me. This is how your father's flirting first started with me
DAD	still working out where to start with you
MAMA	*eh*?
	GRANDDAD *is amused*.
NANA	He looked like he needed a meal. You looked like you needed a meal.
DAD	I needed a meal.
GRANDDAD	He looked like I did.
NANA	You needed more than a meal
DAD	she looked well-fed.
GRANDDAD	Got more than a meal –
MAMA	eh – what?
GRANDDAD	Got more than what I asked for.

JNR SISTER	*What*?
	DAD *is amused*.
GRANDDAD	Got more than –
NANA	don't mind him – don't pay your grandfather no mind – he don't know what he's sayin
GRANDDAD	"I don't know what I'm sayin"?
NANA	He don't know what he's rememberin.
GRANDDAD	"I don't know what I'm rememberin"?
GIRLFRIEND	I'm sayin 'do I look like someone who can't?'
BOYFRIEND	'You look like – '
JNR SISTER	'does she look like someone who can't?'
BOYFRIEND	'You look like someone who could – '
GIRLFRIEND	'do I look like someone who couldn't?'
JNR SISTER	'She doesn't look like someone who / couldn't.'
BOYFRIEND	'You look like someone who should.'
GIRLFRIEND	'I know I don't look like someone who couldn't – '
JNR SISTER	'she don't look like – '
GIRLFRIEND	(*To* SISTER.) *shut up* – (*To* BOYFRIEND.) '…I know I don't look like someone who couldn't…'
BOYFRIEND	'You look like someone who would…'
MAMA	Oh God
BOYFRIEND	' – would cook. Who is able… who has the talent…'
	DAD *is amused*.
DAD	He has the mouth
NANA	he has the mouth.
MAMA	You had the mouth

DAD	I was better.
GIRLS	Were you?
DAD	Still am.
JNR SISTER	Was he?
GRANDDAD	I was better.
NANA	Oh God. Don't mind / him.
GRANDDAD	I was something
NANA	he thought he was / something.
GRANDDAD	still am something
NANA	still thinks he's something
GRANDDAD	she knows exactly what kinda / something –
NANA	don't mind him –
GRANDDAD	forgotten nothing
NANA	forgotten everything
GRANDDAD	and neither have you.
NANA GRANDDAD	
MAMA	Don't mind them.
BOYFRIEND	'The – '
GIRLFRIEND	'what?'
BOYFRIEND	'The – '
JNR SISTER	'what?'
BOYFRIEND	'The – '
NANA	what did he say?
BOYFRIEND	'The – what can I say… The what is there to say? The what is there to say about – you?'
MAMA	Oh God. Mouth.

BOYFRIEND	'The – what is there to say about you?'
DAD	Mouth.
	CHOIR: *The melody of the lament restarts hummed under the following:*
BOYFRIEND	'The what is there left to say about you?
	BOYFRIEND *admires her* CHOIR: *Stops hum of lament. Silence.*
	…Will you?'
	CHOIR: JNR SISTER *is called and lamented by* CHOIR *as she leaves her position on stage, then hummed, underscoring dialogue into next scene.*

Scene Two

A moment as JNR SISTER *leaves.*
CHOIR *underscoring following dialogue with a hummed melody.*

GIRLFRIEND	Askin me – he asked me if I – askin me if I could –
BOYFRIEND	' – able. You are. You / are – able.'
GIRLFRIEND	Thinks he can ask me – thinks he can sweetmouth me with:
BOYFRIEND	'You are – you is – you do – you able – you look you look like – you able to have the ability the capability the capacity – '
GIRLFRIEND	'to what?'

BOYFRIEND	'To…to…'
GIRLFRIEND	He thinks that's going to…?
BOYFRIEND	' – the aptitude. the talent the touch.'
GIRLFRIEND	'The touch?'
BOYFRIEND	'The – you are – you is – you do – you do got – the touch… The sweetness of your touch – '
GIRLFRIEND	'oh God'
BOYFRIEND	'you do – you is – you are – look at you… Look how – look how *sweet* – '
GIRLFRIEND	'*what?*'
BOYFRIEND	'your touch would – could that… / taste.'
MAMA	He asked you if you could cook?
BOYFRIEND	'The calm, the control, the composure you contain – to – '
GIRLFRIEND	'to what?'
BOYFRIEND	'The capabilities you must have to – '
GIRLFRIEND	'to what?'
BOYFRIEND	'to carry out your – '
	CHOIR: *Hummed melody out, sharply.*
MAMA	oh God
BOYFRIEND	'to – cook.'
DAD	I asked you if you / could cook –
MAMA	You knew I could cook –
DAD	can she / cook?
MAMA	which is why you asked me – you knew – he knew –
DAD	she can't cook

MAMA	you knew. Why did you ask? He knew – he knew before he asked – he asked because he did know – Mama ask him –
NANA	why did you ask?
DAD	She looked like she could eat –
	GRANDDAD *is amused*.
MAMA	*that's* your father.
DAD	A well-fed woman. *That's* my wife.
NANA	*My* daughter –
GRANDDAD	our well-fed daughter.
DAD	But can she cook?
	GIRLFRIEND *says nothing*.
	She doesn't cook.
MAMA	I coached her to cook. Coached them to…
GIRLFRIEND	Why would I cook?
DAD	Why doesn't she cook?
GIRLFRIEND	Mama cooks… Mama cooks, what I eat.
MAMA	They learnt their cooking capabilities from me.
NANA	*I* coached you to cook –
MAMA	I –
NANA	I did. I was the cooker – you was the cookless –
GRANDDAD	you couldn't cook.
GIRLFRIEND	Nana couldn't cook?
DAD	Your mother couldn't cook?
MAMA	Course she could cook –
NANA	– I couldn't cook?
MAMA	Mama could cook

NANA	I couldn't cook?
MAMA	Course she could cook – she coached me – and he knows it
GRANDDAD	you couldn't cook either.
GIRLFRIEND	
GRANDDAD	I coached her. I coached her too. *That's* your… She was a bad learner.
NANA	…Don't mind him. Don't pay him no mind.
MAMA NANA MAMA	
GIRLFRIEND	He asked me if I could cook, Mama –
GRANDDAD	he asked *her* – if she could *cook*?
	GRANDDAD *is amused*.
MAMA	This is how they start –
NANA	oh.
DAD	Have to start somewhere
MAMA	oh.
	GRANDDAD *laughs*.
	This is how your father started with me.
NANA	This is how your father started with me.
MAMA	This is how your father flirted with me. This is how your father's flirting started with me
DAD	still working out where to start with you
MAMA	*eh?*
	GRANDDAD *is amused*.
NANA	He looked like he needed a meal. You looked like you needed a meal.
DAD	I needed a meal.

GRANDDAD	He looked like I did.
NANA	You needed more than a meal
DAD	she looked well-fed.
GRANDDAD	Got more than a meal –
MAMA	eh – what?
GRANDDAD	Got more than I asked.

DAD *is amused*.

Got more than –

NANA	don't mind him – don't pay your grandfather no…
GRANDDAD	"I don't know what I'm sayin"
NANA	He don't know what he's / rememberin.
GRANDDAD	"I don't know what I'm rememberin".

CHOIR: *Hummed melody of lament underscores the following:*

GIRLFRIEND	I'm sayin – 'do I look like someone who can't?'
BOYFRIEND	'You look like – you look like someone who could – '
GIRLFRIEND	'do I look like someone who / couldn't?'
BOYFRIEND	'You look like someone who should.'
GIRLFRIEND	'I know I don't look like someone who / wouldn't – '
BOYFRIEND	'You look like someone who would…'
MAMA	Oh God
BOYFRIEND	' – cook. Who is able… who has the talent…'

DAD *is amused*.

DAD	He has the / mouth.
NANA	He has the mouth.
MAMA	You had the mouth

DAD	I was better.
GIRLFRIEND	Were you?
DAD	Still am.
GRANDDAD	I was better.
NANA	Oh God. Don't mind / him.
GRANDDAD	I was something
NANA	he thought he was / something.
GRANDDAD	still am something
NANA	still thinks he's something
GRANDDAD	she knows exactly what kinda / something –
NANA	don't mind him –
GRANDDAD	forgotten nothing
NANA	forgotten everything
GRANDDAD	and neither have you.
GRANDDAD NANA	
MAMA	Don't mind them.
BOYFRIEND	'The – '
GIRLFRIEND	'what?'
BOYFRIEND	'The – '
NANA	what did he say?
BOYFRIEND	'The – what can I say… The what is there to say? The what is there to say about you?'
MAMA	Oh God. Mouth.
BOYFRIEND	'The – what is there to say about you?'
DAD	Mouth.
BOYFRIEND	'The what is there left to say about you…?

CHOIR: *Humming of lament out. Silence.*

...Will you?'

CHOIR: BOYFRIEND *and* GIRLFRIEND
are called and lamented by CHOIR *as they
leave their positions.*

Scene Three

BOYFRIEND *and* GIRLFRIEND *leave.*
Scene starts with cast dialogue only, CHOIR *silent.*

MAMA   He asked her if she could cook.
            Oh God.

DAD   I asked you if you could / cook –

MAMA   You knew I could / cook –

DAD   could she cook?

MAMA   Which is why you asked me – you knew – he
            knew –

DAD   she couldn't cook.

MAMA   You knew. Why did you ask? He knew – you
            knew before he asked – he asked because he
            did know – Mama ask / him –

NANA   Why did you ask?

DAD   She looked like she could eat.

            GRANDDAD *is amused.*

MAMA   *That's* their father.

DAD   A well-fed woman. *That's* my / wife.

NANA   *My* daughter –

GRANDDAD   our well-fed daughter.

DAD   Could she cook?
            She didn't / cook.

MAMA	I coached her to cook. Coached them / to cook.
DAD	Why didn't she cook?
MAMA	They learnt their capabilities / from me.
NANA	*I* coached you to cook – I did. I was the cooker – I was the cooker who coached the cookless. I coached you to / cook –
GRANDDAD	You couldn't cook.
DAD	Your mother couldn't / cook?
MAMA	Course she could cook –
NANA	I couldn't cook?
MAMA	Mama could / cook
NANA	I couldn't cook?
MAMA	Dada, Mama could cook. Course she could cook – she coached me – and he knows / it.
GRANDDAD	You couldn't cook either. I coached her. I coached you too…
MAMA	
GRANDDAD	She was a bad learner.
NANA	Don't mind him. Don't pay him no mind.
MAMA NANA MAMA	
	CHOIR: *Solo female voice of* CHOIR *hums a lament melody underscoring the following dialogue:*
GRANDDAD	He asked her if she could cook.
MAMA	…This is how they start –
NANA	oh.
DAD	Have to start somewhere

MAMA	oh. This is how you started with me.
NANA	This is how your father started with me.
MAMA	This is how you flirted with – (me). This is how your flirting started / with me.
DAD	Still working out where to start with you
MAMA	*eh?*
NANA	He looked like he needed a meal. You looked like you needed a meal.
DAD	I needed a / meal.
GRANDDAD	He looked like I did.
NANA	You needed more than a meal
DAD	she looked well-fed.
GRANDDAD	Got more than a meal – got more than / I asked –
NANA	Don't mind him – don't pay your Father no mind –
GRANDDAD	"I don't know what I'm sayin."
NANA	You don't know what you're / rememberin.
GRANDDAD	"I don't know what I'm rememberin."
MAMA	Oh God.
DAD	He had the mouth
NANA	he had the mouth.
MAMA	You had the mouth
DAD	I was better. Still am.
MAMA	
GRANDDAD	I was better.
NANA	Oh God. Don't mind / him.

GRANDDAD	I was something
NANA	he thinks he's / something
GRANDDAD	still am something
NANA	still thinks he's something
GRANDDAD	she knows exactly what kinda / something –
NANA	don't mind him –
GRANDDAD	forgotten nothing
NANA	forgotten everything
GRANDDAD	and neither have you.
NANA GRANDDAD	

CHOIR: *Lament out.*

MAMA	Don't mind them.
DAD	This thing.
NANA	What did he say?
DAD	I miss them.
NANA	What did he say?
MAMA	Oh God. Mouth.
DAD	Mouth.

CHOIR: DAD *is called and lamented by the* CHOIR *as he leaves his position. The hummed lament kicks back in.*

Scene Four

A moment as DAD *leaves.*
CHOIR*: Hummed lament underscores the following:*

MAMA	He asked her if she could cook? Oh God. He knew I could cook – which is why he asked me – he knew – that's why he asked – Mama asked him why he asked – Mama asked him… That's why he asked.
	CHOIR*: Lament out.*
NANA MAMA	
MAMA	*That* was their father… …I coached her to cook. Coached them to cook. They learnt their cooking capabilities / from me.
NANA	I coached you to cook –
MAMA	I –
NANA	I did. I was the cooker – you was the cookless – I was the cooker who coached the cookless… I coached you to cook… You were a / bad learner –
GRANDDAD	You couldn't cook
MAMA	course she / could cook –
NANA	I couldn't cook?
MAMA	Mama could / cook
NANA	I couldn't cook?
MAMA	Dada… Mama could cook. She coached me… and you / know it –
GRANDDAD	You couldn't cook either. I coached her. I coached her too. That's your mother.
MAMA	

GRANDDAD	She was a / bad learner.
NANA	Don't mind him. Don't pay him no… (mind.)
MAMA	
NANA	
MAMA	
	CHOIR: *Lament in, underscoring the following:*
GRANDDAD	He asked her if she could cook.
MAMA	That's how they started –
NANA	oh.
MAMA	This is how he started with me.
NANA	This is how your father started with me.
MAMA	This is how he flirted with me. This is how his flirting / started with me.
NANA	He looked like he needed a meal. You looked like you needed / a meal.
GRANDDAD	He looked like I / did.
NANA	You needed more than a meal. I fed her well.
GRANDDAD	Got more than a meal –
MAMA	eh – what?
GRANDDAD	Got more than / I asked.
NANA	Don't pay your father no mind… he doesn't know / what he's…
GRANDDAD	I don't know what I'm sayin… I don't know what I'm rememberin…
MAMA	Oh God.
NANA	He had the mouth.
MAMA	He had the mouth. He was good.
NANA	Oh God.
GRANDDAD	I was / something

NANA	Don't mind him.
GRANDDAD	…Still am something.
NANA	Still thinks he's / something
GRANDDAD	She knows exactly what kinda something – forgotten nothing
NANA	forgotten everything
GRANDDAD	…And neither have you.
NANA	
GRANDDAD	
	CHOIR: *Lament out.*
NANA	This thing.
MAMA	Don't mind me.
NANA	This big dying thing.
GRANDDAD	What did she say?
MAMA	I miss them.
NANA	What did she say?
MAMA	Oh God. Mouth.

CHOIR: MAMA *is called and lamented by* CHOIR *as she leaves her position.*

Scene Five

A moment as MAMA *leaves.*
The CHOIR *is silent.*

NANA   *I* coached her to cook – I did… I was the cooker – she was the cookless – I was the cooker who coached the cookless… I… coached her to (cook)… She was a bad learner.

Beat

GRANDDAD	You couldn't cook.
NANA	I couldn't cook? I couldn't cook.
GRANDDAD	She couldn't (cook) either… …I coached her. I coached her too. That's our – was our… she was our… She was a bad learner.
NANA GRANDDAD	
NANA	Don't pay it no mind. She didn't pay you no… (mind)
GRANDDAD NANA	
NANA	He asked her if she could cook. Oh. …This is how you started with me. You looked like you needed / a meal.
GRANDDAD	I needed a meal.
	Beat.
NANA	You needed more than / a meal.
GRANDDAD	Got more than a meal.
NANA	
GRANDDAD	Got more than I asked. Got more than… Thank you.
NANA	
NANA	Do you know what you're saying?
GRANDDAD	
GRANDDAD	…I know what I'm saying… And I remember.
NANA	He had the mouth.

GRANDDAD	Was I better?
NANA	Oh God.
GRANDDAD	I was something.
NANA	I think you're something.
GRANDDAD	Still am something.
NANA	You are.
GRANDDAD	Forgotten nothing.
NANA	
GRANDDAD	...No. And neither have you.
NANA GRANDDAD	
GRANDDAD	This thing. This dying thing... This unease. This dis-ease.
NANA	I miss them.
NANA GRANDDAD	
GRANDDAD	...What did he say?
	What did he say?
NANA	

Both looking for those that have gone.

Oh God.
Oh God.

Oh God.

End.

www.nickhernbooks.co.uk

facebook.com/nickhernbooks

twitter.com/nickhernbooks